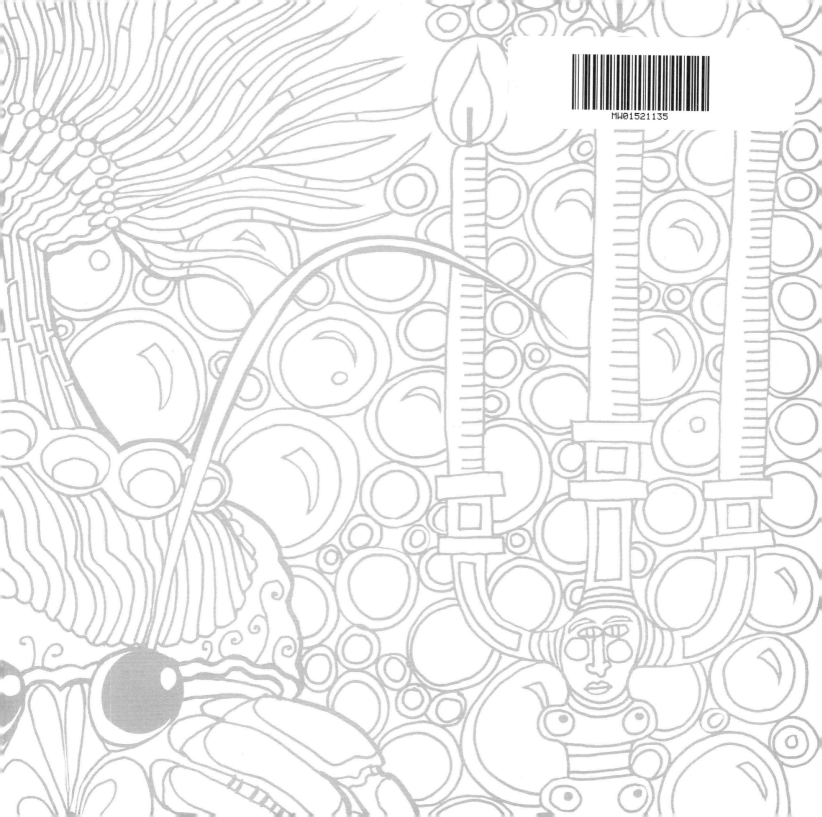

Tangle Bay

AN ENCHANTING COLOURING
BOOK WITH HIDDEN TREASURE

Jessica Palmer

Dedication

For Jessie Mary Birkhead (1985–2015),
who loved drawing and colouring.
And my beloved Ben, Katie and Keith.

First published in 2016

Search Press Limited, Welwood, North Farm Road,
Tunbridge Wells, Kent, TN2 3DR

Text and illustration copyright © Jessica Palmer, 2016

Design copyright © Search Press, 2016

ISBN: 978-1-78221-413-7

Printed in China

This book belongs to:

....

You are invited to visit the Facebook page:
Tangle Wood Colouring Book, where you can post
your coloured images.

Why not also set up a colouring club? Get together
with friends and share pens, pencils and all the
fun of colouring.

Welcome to Tangle Bay

Are you ready for some fun at the beach? Come and play in a wonderful seaside place full of dancing dolphins, surfing puffins and spirals of shells. This is an enchanted world where mermaids chase through the tangles of the deep and sailing ships are tossed on bubbling waves. Scattered through the hand-drawn illustrations, you will discover lost treasures. Try tinting them with a gold pen. In a rock pool, over the horizon, on the sand under a moonlit sky – this is a place to play with colour. Add your own creative splash to the open spaces. Come and dive down into the deep, relax in the sun or sail away – to Tangle Bay.

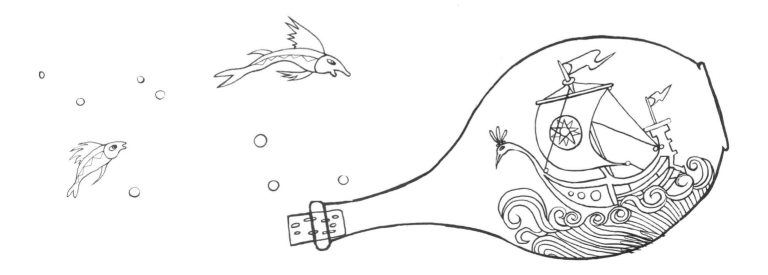

These are some of the treasures buried
in Tangle Bay:

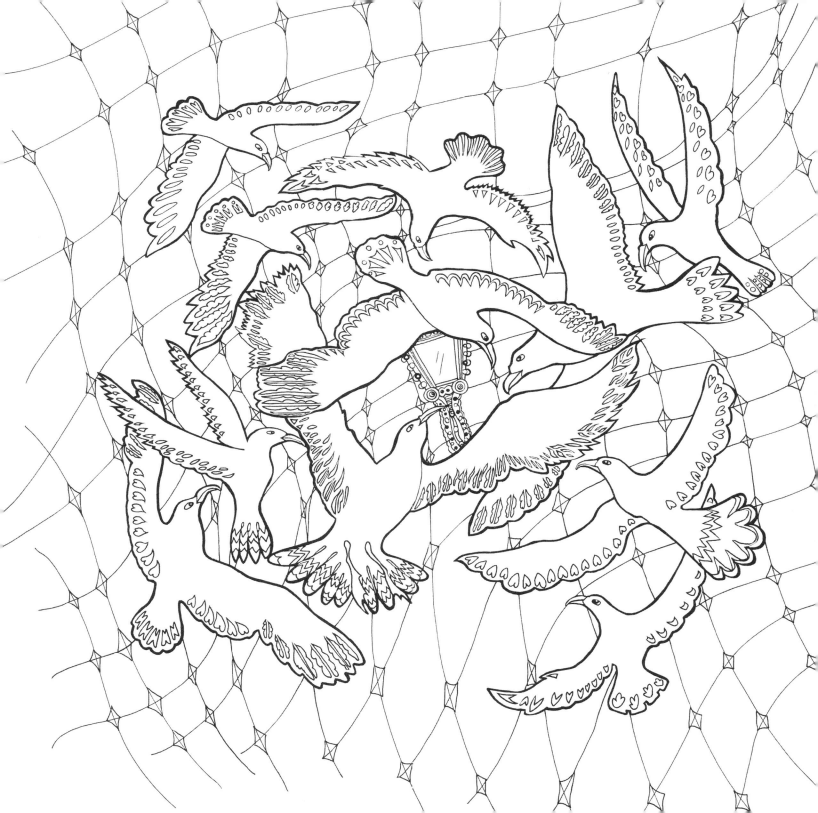

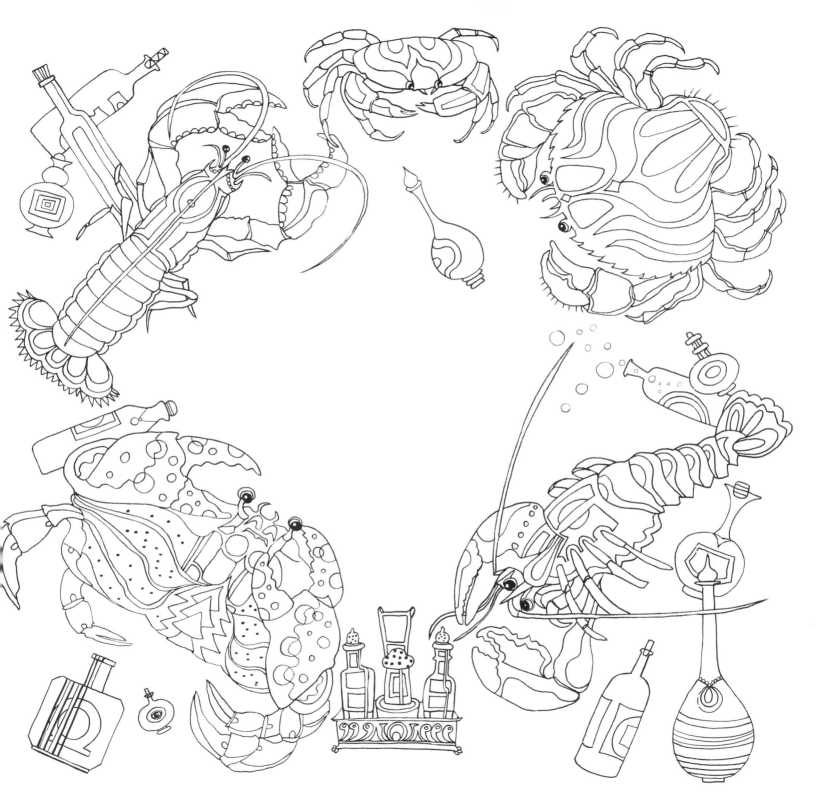

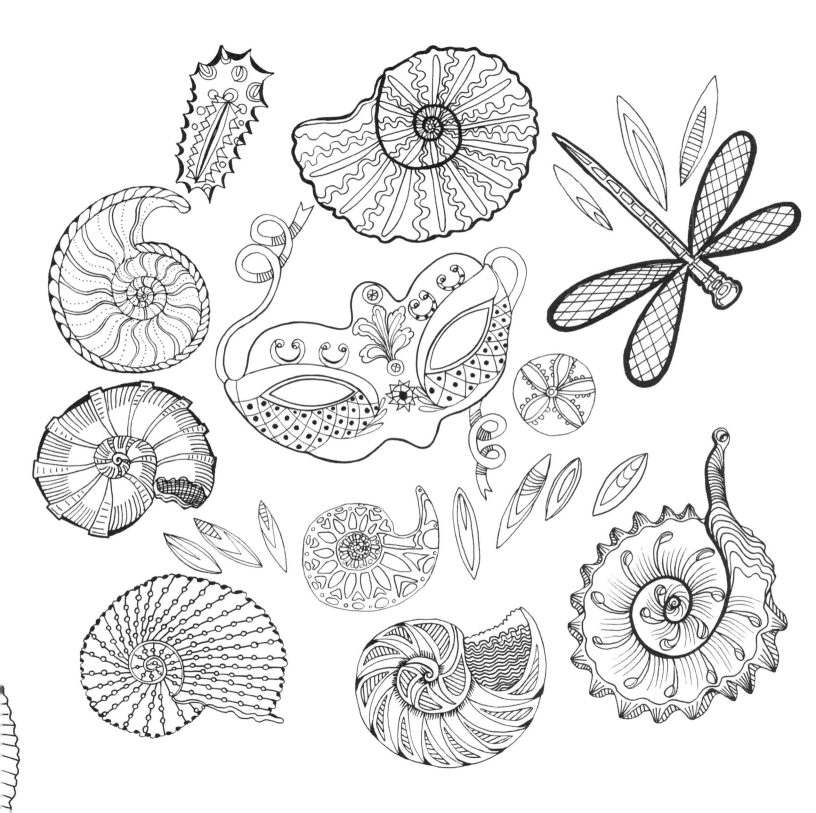

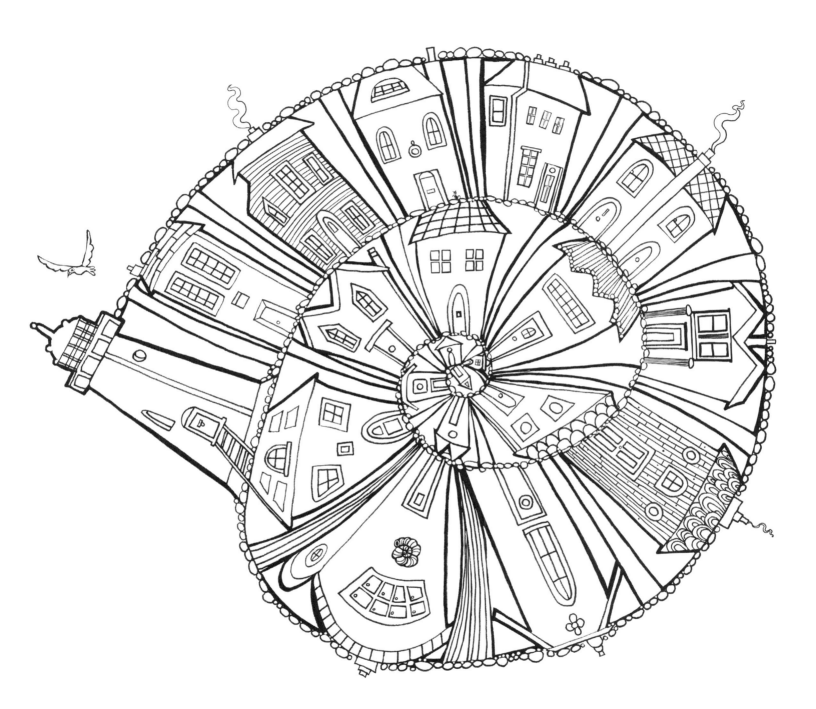

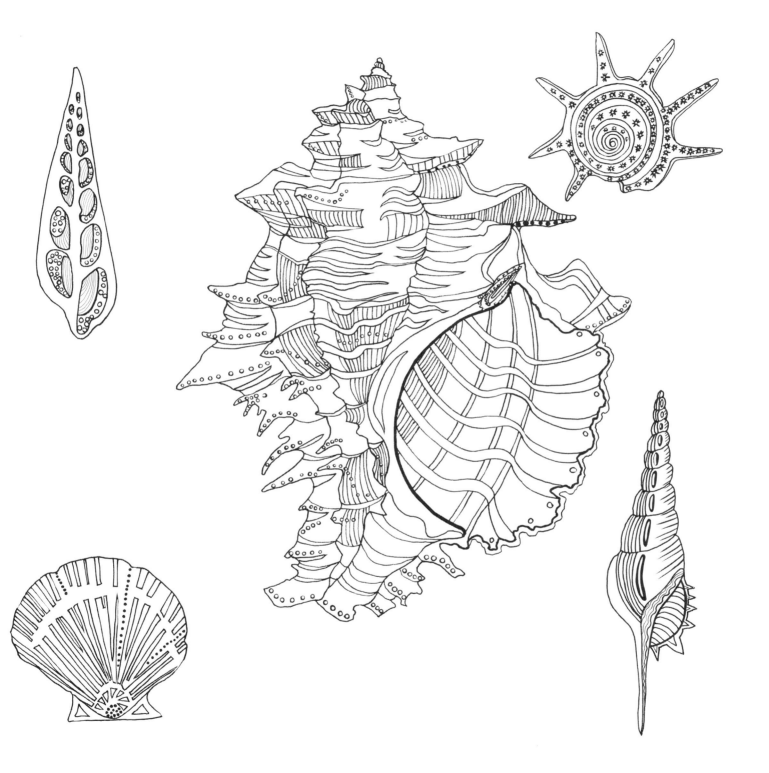

TANGLE BAY

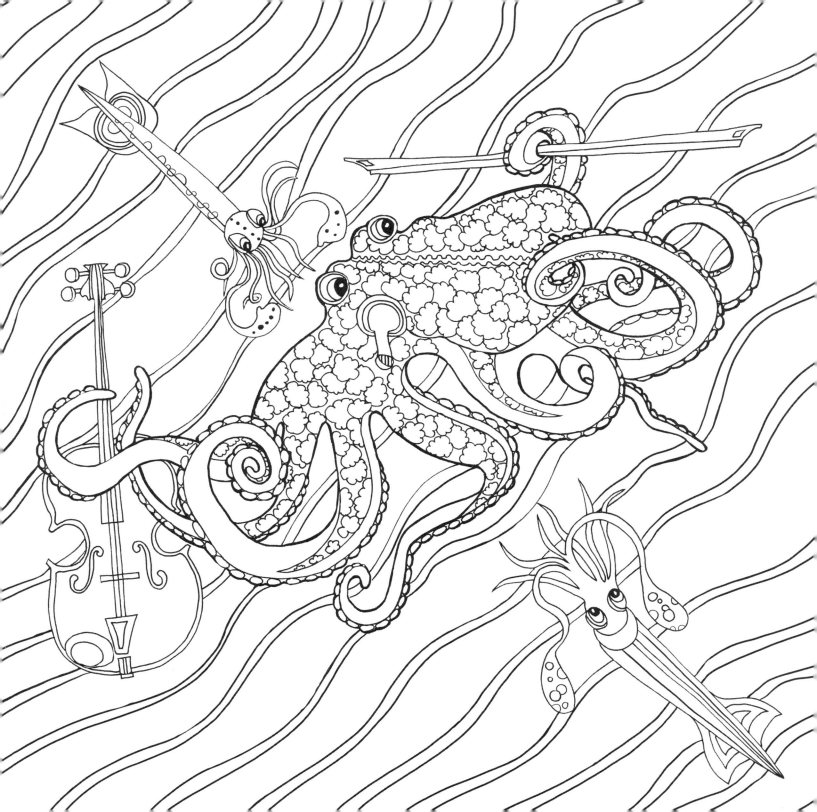

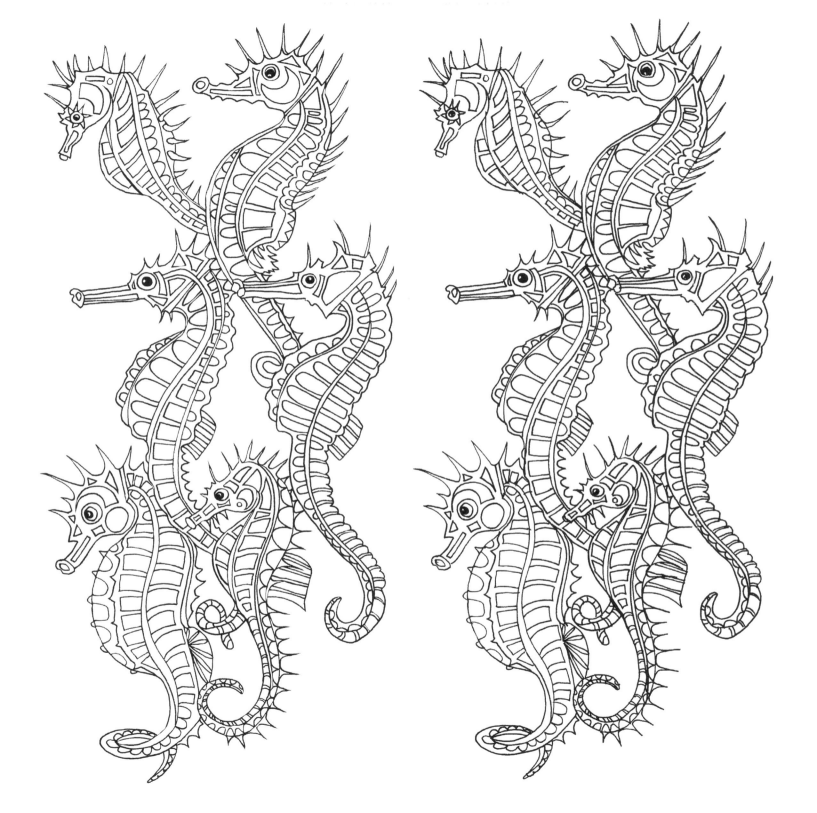